PAREIDOLIA

Pareidolia

ISBN 9780645797732

Walleah Press
South Launceston
Tasmania, Australia 7249

www.walleahpress.com.au
ralph.wessman@walleahpress.com.au

PAREIDOLIA

Ed Southorn

CONTENTS

EDOUARD ETIENNE LEVIER

Glazed eyes sunk under squid lids
Cannot fit me the watcher
Keen to make curious sense of you
This gaudy pale dilettante

Together we share a name along the line
Alone in an empty room full of secrets
No experience nor custom nor thought
The same to recognize or cast on

I persevere squatting on my perch
Hypnotised by the mystery of identity
Peering hungrily close at an Other
Tricked up in check like Sherlock

The linguist who became of all things
A hatter and maybe even so they say
Before Melbourne a gun runner
Wrapped in velvet I suspect
Unnoticed like Rimbaud

Worshipped at the ancestral shrine
Are you idol conscience hero
Rival I am swaying blind
Were you thinking of me as I of you

Waiting for a shot of recognition
Blast of cognition flash of intuition
Until that revelatory moment
When the model blinks back
Everyone else freezes you

Remain as you knew you would be
Deliberately mute and yet
Did you wonder who will remember
Who will gaze on your impassive face
In the sorry future

Neither knows who the other might be
Am I what you wished we might become
Nothing I got nothing
But I do know one thing about you
Something you would never see

In absentia you are tangibly present
Unlike after you looked back at the lens
Frozen ponce feet up in that soft chair
Contrived amid brazen sangfroid

CANE TOADS

Why have they not been caramelised
until approaching essence, good
as mercury or hash oil?

Forget Vegemite on sourdough,
why do we not prefer them
to set the twilight reeling?

They say they came from Maui,
agents of the Rainbow Bridge,
hallucinogens after all are sacred.

But no, four iron Armageddon,
wrath of gleeful crusaders,
or plastic bag euthanasia,
sputters down upon them.

Knobby glazed pork buns
peering out from the deep freeze
for a trippy chef,
these are their preferred
fates and furies,
they like it this way,
haphazard piecemeal harvest
is encouragement.

Thousands are sacrificed,
millions more grow unmolested
waiting to be singled out
so they too can die like martyrs,
extending the line across
all known territory.

BLUE DUET

Outside, Gotham's black night trembles. Cut it
down, let the gargoyle punk loose. Something
that sinister will fly to the Devil's Lair. All
I need do is speed unseen in the shadows. Gone
across the river, follow the mad jester's tune.
Our nemesis is out there, always recording

his every violent, pathetic debacle. Recording?
Oh yes, you mumbling, cowering scapegoat. Cut it
on the pasty white flesh of my fans, it's something
I've evolved over lifetimes of vengeance. Gone
are my ruddy looks, but this bright smile is not all

I am. Oh no, ha ha, never, not once at all.
Scapegoat? I'm more your measure than any recording
can reveal. You cheapshot, your fury aims to see me gone
but you've never beaten me. You're mine to cut, it
makes no difference what mask you wear. Something
to keep me on my toes, run my engine in tune,

that's all you are. Yet, I ruefully admit, another tune.
A nickel, son, to scan your ledger, faces many and all
they fill my screen perpetually, as if something
else, not your sorry soul, is secretly recording
our combat, so although I beat you down, you never cut it
out. One of you, or another, you're never gone.

At the end, after the clash, I'm melancholy gone
picking blue notes in my rocking chair, any old tune.
Mask discarded, really I just don't cut it.
So many downtrodden, but so few of y'all
rise up, strike back. Only some are recording
making the same song over, yet something

cool and smooth in all your sweet gone tune
leaves the recording act supremely defiant.
After you've cut it, something new survives.

JABREEN

Yugambeh Country
with respect

Out of warm caldera, canoe.
Black snake hair, purple berry eyes,
callistemon beard. Jabreen is hunting.

Sea eagle clears waxy scrub, aims
back at the sun. I search along the golden
bank, find only drag marks.

He drains the honey bag, raises up the bluff.
I am his languid blink. Stuck on slippery,
I turn to the sound of lizard voices.

At night he climbs to the hidden cave.
River is a net, stars campfires.
Crows burn black. I hear them throw
stones, bringing fish.

Tide fills until I see moon become
nautilus shell. Magpies warble, tip the sky
open. Sunup spurts rain like laughter.

I am lost in perplexed longing.
Spear clips my ear. His story retold past
rock time, perhaps he was merciful after all.

PIPPA'S HAIR

Her name was cool, at that time
But now gorgeous Pippa seems
Well, faintly ridiculous
Big blue eyes, red pouty lips, splash of freckles
Strawberry blonde hair like ropey silk
Her shiny hair was a talisman
If she had lost her hair, the spell would be broken
I stood at the top of the Balnarring track
Surprised to see her, just the two of us
Light rain, a quiet beach, deserted I had thought
She waved far below, signalling
For me to go ahead, her waiting hair
Shining in the littoral gloom
I took one step and fell, sliding down
Letting go my board, wetsuit muddy
Bumping the footholds, trying to grasp
Branches, leaves, vines looking,
Feeling like rope but I could not grab hold
I tumbled, spun and landed at her feet
She bent down to offer me her
Hand and I reaching up
With dirty, bleeding hand
Gently held her hair

PAREIDOLIA

This vision we project to make the seeming
Inanimate look back at us is far beyond a
Linnaeus label locking away the wonder
We recognise after ages of accretion
More than a laboratory exchange
Making Rorschach imagery
Like the watchman who says
I'm not here with you
You're here with me

It is recognition of the rainbow storm to calm
Unlocked from our hearts
Given form to flit
Across this shield this magnet this mirror
Because if you look into a pair of eyes
Approaching in the street
You may well see one offers
Kindness the other as if to say
Don't be ridiculous

An arrangement of molecules
Across bark or bones pulled this way or that
Turning submission into rejection loss back
To hope by the faintest barely perceptible
Was it ever there or not twitch and flex
Whim of lip full of luscious promise one second
Drained to perdition the next
Is the puppet mistress making shadow from muscle

This echo of right brain left brain
Is sentenced to remain
Tension coiled in the eyes

Unseen by each other
Riven by sheer cliffs
Twinning physics of the soul
When you looked at me
Your eyes harmonised

AT LAST

Miss Alice B. is ready for delivery
In her layers of Egyptian cotton
Polish amber hanging below
Her concealed throat
Like the flotsam on the rocks
Under the cargo wharf
She doesn't look at him
Gleaming half naked
Muscles like wrapped rigging
He gently lifts her
Up and over the side
A tender exotic flower
He must preserve
She is ugly, he thinks, the face
Faintly scaled and milky like
A lizard's belly and the lips
Dry and thin as a dead worm
He is a man after all and like all men
He must be treated, she supposes
Like a dog, carefully and with
Condescending affection
Etched against the morning horizon
The arriviste and the indigene
Aware of the possibility of disaster
Neither able to withdraw
The ship creaks and echoes
And for a moment that is all
She brushes her skirts
Raises her eyes at last
In a different light

ST GEORGES ROAD

Teasing behind proud trees
Glittering wealth comports

Inside the plush fortress who knew
Such terror desire bursting

From black hearts who heard crashing
Glass so cruel without compass

Who will be witness to those
Gently laying pistols on polished

Chiffonier ripping drawers scattering silver
Choosing the carving knife snarling like lions

Wine spilling from crystal stuffing mouths
With linen and lace taking their good time

A sporting weekly flapped across the lawn
Baron Ruthven on the cover punting

Arms wide floating above the Junction Oval
Lefty rover glint in his eye never a hair

Out of place when they were found
No one noticed who had fallen back to Earth

RENDEZVOUS

Seeds dropped on unbroken ground
Sound of growth undiminished
Until undeterred irresistible
Without restraint I go up

Fear becomes pride comforting
Sweet implacable resinous
Quickens the heart into temptation

Gold eggs gold coins clamour
Magic harp nothing beside unsullied
Elixir of escape I am enlarged

Gog turns and smiles sweetly
Takes grapes from my smooth hand
Nothing else to bring only calm and quiet

All is calm even the wind like reassurance
Closer to the great curve
Not privileged nor fleeing discipline
Unlike the *Baron in the Trees*

Deep underground the giver sighs
A warning I reply in a language
I cannot know but of course
I think I understand perfectly

I murmur now although back then
Up so high I suspected nothing
Close to a state of entelechy
Dealing cards in the clouds

SECOND AMENDMENT

The trigger fires off a despatch
Roiling along paths deep
Enough to deceive

Flies soon gather and skit
Heavy as silken thread
Careless beyond reproach

He looks up from the plate
Chaotic disciples led by
Their own unsquared feast

Crumbs falling like bombs
Runs his tongue along teeth
Collapsing like cliffs
Tasting fragrance of gun metal

THE IDIOT

He picks someone in the crowd
Someone he has never met

Salutes with a wax finger
As if to say I know you

I recognise your contribution
But I know nothing about you

I do not care for what
You might have done

I cannot deny I might turn
Cold on you my embrace

Might turn you to scum
Under the white glare

Here is where ideology
Engulfs the state

Science is the apostate
Where views are framed

By desire to resist where
Those not with him

Are meaningless to him
He has known this space

For some time now
But his resistance insists

On refusing to examine
What and who he knows

How much he might lose
Dry winds rush the stage

He turns back once more
Grimacing thumbs up

Hearty as one may be
Covered in wax

Before stepping off
Eyes melting down

Some consolation
So paltry really

BEHEMOTH

After STC

Lost souls plead like wasted emissaries
Tainted by the great unquenched
Faces so gnarled in a mirror surely
A vision from the Bay of Vanished Hope
Charts and instruments take flight

Guiding themselves to hysterical oblivion
Bulgakov's cat leans back unperturbed
Cursorily puffing a cigar in the captain's chair
Outside pointing to the twinkling blanket of salvation
A rack upon which is lashed the patched dirty

Linen of a wastrel creaks in the foul wind
Sailors gather round yet do not bargain
They prosecute hatred like foul meat
Sticking in the cracks oh wonder oh sorrow
Too late now the whimpering has begun

The rocking stops becalmed tears
Sweat gleam on a writhing slimy sea
The bird is placed the dice rolled they gag
One the number there like a ghost
Thump and thump knocking on

If they knew they might still choose
This way the way they dream
He lets the glow go out
Wraps his tail licks his paw
Glances at the dice does not blink

EMPHYSEMA

We emerged but we urge to go back re-enter
Unfathomable fragrant as invisible life
On the rocks at low tide
It is with us always all around us
What floats on it can only be carried by it
The element that perpetuates its dying relies
Upon it to create the very poison nevertheless

Storing the past silent like a library
Inscrutable repository of secrets
Ages when it was the only way in and out
The only way to know anything be anywhere
Its own cosmos own triumphs
Humiliations heroes of the great fleet
Rogues killers colonisers drifting

Weightless with desire flickering into view
Retreating into shadow obscured immeasurably
Heavy energy that could save us but cannot be
Turned on or off or told anything at all
Sending rain flood fire famine escapees
Giving up bringing down we hanker to live
Beside it yet do not value it enough

We cannot reconcile or realise why we will
Never know what we have done
There is nothing we can do
No medicine left
The patient has emphysema
The skin cannot breathe

ANCESTRAL

They are raised up to die
These glorious swimmers
Perfect flashing bodies
Smooth to the end
Retrieved but never caught
Laid gently in caskets
Loaded aboard hearses
Docking like space ships
Shooting to other planets
Oil and spark
Slip and slide
Going down
Flesh unto flesh

DEAR LEADER

A conga line of immodest BMWs
Red hibiscus shirt snap back
Moleskins greeted by charcoal

Charred wrecks of old Valiants
Fused tractors seething wraiths
Howling screaming roaring hands

Shaking no hands to shake
Judgement not a mark on paper
Words on a screen now shouted

At a camera words become smoke
I reach out my hand not a hand up
Or any comfort I reach out my hand

Hoping to find humanity
Have some of it rub off
My smirk a puzzled frown

Twisted becomes a grimace
I give praise to reassure myself
See only myself in the landscape

Others mere shadows
Or opportunities to contrast
I do not have a mask my guilt

Cannot be filtered
My face lit up is best hidden
Eyes lowered gaze averted

You would think this the devil's work
I an ally of Mephistopheles
It is another merciful not merciful

Vast and terrible my fate alone
I will never stand beside warriors
No man of the hour I am a dissembler

Excuse maker buck passer blame shifter
I cannot conjure like Prospero
Do not recognise Dante's way out

I try again to reassure myself the louder
I shout the more foolish I sound
I have made uneasy peace with fools

Dangerous because they do not recognise
Danger fusing illogic popping and curling
Brown and black still too hot to touch

Sure I can fix this using
Others' strength and knowledge
To help myself my faith

Echoes ersatz in a big box shed glib
Reassurance until my hypocrisy shatters
Someone else's responsibility

My confected empathy misunderstood
By myself I deny and insist proudly
Defending a miracle only I can see

WILDSONG

How far did his heart fall, that moment he realised
he'd missed the boat? Did it fall slowly, juggled
by the wind, or did it plummet and crash? How to
manage the next hours, the long months?
When hope is lost, how long until new hope?
He rode in his mind across the ice arriving at a place
called Certainty, where time is not allowed.

Feather light marathon, the other pole measured
in degrees of exhaustion, recovery riding in
Pleiades, hiding in the wind, not a word
spoken. Noisy million glances, nods exchanged,
they return every year so long after Magellan,
approaching the meaning of wait, balancing
the long or short of a cause, floating forgotten,
invisible. Rhythm and melody making wildsong
on shoals of composure.

THE WALK OUT

Stepping down flinging the back page the door opens in the window turquoise clear ahead I was so long uncoiled governed by the need to provide against the slide I rubbed shoulders with the keys but nah that's done all done I don't go into the office and fight for a chair that won't fuck up my back come back and it's gone innocently across the floor I walk out the door throw my arms up and declare I am not there I am nowhere I am following clouds and trees and steep shadowed paths and steps too deep to take in easy steps I must case the next step not stepping in time I have paid a price as if those first ten years stepping away rising at dawn breathing in the sky wishing and finding waves rising smooth as old sanded paint for me often enough for me knowing even as I slid away in humble elation others confined every day watched and counted me out and yet by year four or five I turned less flexed less limbs and eyes straightened out saw it was harder than before I crab walked on one good leg up to the jump off pushed off arms leather straps clinging not pumping I walked back to the car blood trickling down my brow my shin skin flapping on the big toe of my left foot oblivious who tried to faintly mock as decorously as he might so utterly unaware I had no idea cared not felt not wondered only how to slate thirst and hunger I might be unable to shout what's important is a dry towel a car park and good music.

LOVIN' NOBODY BUT YOU

No couple can do this
Undeniably natural like that
Anniversaries come and go
They never celebrate
Their eternal bond
Something happened
To them both together
Before coming of age
Together they lose shape
Gain form as walkers
Stop and stare blankly
The unashamed freakshow
Well, yes, like those
Sharing essential internals
Below entwined exchanging
Data enhancing one another
Hard grinding light brushing
Sending it up the ladder
Twice as strong together
This unshakeable hot spot
Signpost of silent stillest
Untamed slow drama so
Happy together

LAMPETIE

I put my hand on your face
The sacred act of touching

Folds pleats veils
Conceal a slow stream

Dark syrup under the bark
Sticks on my raw fingers

Warm and thick these
Folds I will lick so deep

You cannot be exposed
My time of dying is

Longer than your living
Here before and hereafter

My face tells no time
Your conscience like my face

Grows or wilts in good time
From the upturned palm

Lovers gift me their names
My skin like feathers or fur

Marble or washboard
Hard or soft as seed

Engulfs them all
A constellation shuffling

In my own orbit I am
Strong enough to bind

The weight of the world
Nodding to the slightest ripple

I look up and see your
Hair floating wild

Shining green and free
Waving in the dark

Washed by the moon
Blown up and out by

All the great storms
To make us quiver

ODE TO BILL MURRAY

He looked up at the trees
White sun squinting a tattoo

In his eye each one helpless
Decent and strong like

The children of farmers
Nothing they can do made him

Feel much better about
The buffet smothered in dipping

Sauce spa benches stained and
Splintered creche roosters

In purple polyester muttering
Depravities a parade of life size

Glass dogs in the street gallery
They had decided no door charge

For the glass dogs
This fable of his did not last

The small stuff local wildlife
Exotic weeds all burned off

Sifted flour topsoil blown away
Not much left inside

The towers grim knives
Blade up glinting echoes

Rooms with the same Edo print
All empty only a chimpanzee

In a bellboy costume
Bounced around the lobby

In the penthouse seated
On a capacious orange red

Zig zag bed melancholy lonely
His personal assistant

Bound together in a pencil skirt
So tight she fell more than she

Cared to admit blank staring out
The window at the trees

A hollow reprieve dull
Brass walls mirrored ceilings

Patrolling a milky way carpet
Into a cavern of brown stalactite

Chandeliers bandits pinging lives
Shattered indiscriminate careless

Monotony with soft green tables
Long nights on the bed staring

Out the window she's gone
To Manila telling brothers and

Sisters nieces and nephews
That sad gangster he sold

To private equity five hundred
Rooms on the chopping block

The watchers smiled and
Nodded imperceptibly

Anxious gently
Waving their leaves

He came down walked among the
Shadows picking fallen leaves

To weave a sail boat

SHELL RELIQUARY

Caressed with a reverence reserved
For jewels handed down
Each season passing the pairing
The huddle the spilling chosen
By a child's hand sticky with ice cream
Or one whose salt dry wrinkles give
The most careful consideration for mood
Or sentiment let go like a poet placing
Words so as not to upset the apple cart

Tossed on distant waves echoing
Around the perimeter like cyclists
Whirring in a velodrome refuge place
Of blazoned memories snuggled into a
Monkey grip or drawers in a bureau
Where the space of the hidden drawers
Once opened disappears only the sound
Of stones weeping back and forth
On the sea floor

TED HOPKINS

At half time my father drove our red Holden ute
To the park for respite
We kicked the polished leather ball
My kicks desultory dragging a tide of grief
Biggest game of the year a massacre
The heroes all there but not there
Gould Crosswell Nicholls Jesaulenko
Powers muted by cruel gods
I could not be any one of them could not thread
The ball between the trees nothing to be said
Hand on the shoulder accepting fate
We drove home in our chariot of the vanquished
Everyone knew the red ute
The streets were empty we rode alone

I could not resist the cruel dial turning us back
Agony of the call the unceasing roar rising and falling
Like the wave tossed sea I was praying for them
Gould Crosswell Nicholls Jesaulenko
Here was another I had come on they were calling
My name when the prize dropped there I was scouting the pack
Darting into the open goal again and again
Later that evening we watched and saw unmistakeably me
Blonde mop long sleeves socks down opportunist finisher

Barassi jumped the fence perched by the thud
The heckle the pounding of hooves
At the victory blast leapt to his feet head thrown back
Eyes at the clouds arms stretching out for the gods
But that long ago day was not for gods or heroes
Something shifted on the great plane and nothing would be

The same again like Priam reasoning with Achilles
Sleight of hand and a leather ball
Take the boy back risen with his mates
Red ute stabled in the carport grill wide
Eyed teeth bare bloody sword in scabbard

CATHEDRAL

Desperate breath in dry dust light,
your old red coat draped above the altar
because worshipful was the least we could be.
Prone on a steel girder,
vertical against rough pine.
It has come now to this:
mud bath in a brackish reach,
on a rotting log in Tallebudgera Creek
watched over by crows.
We never did anything by half.
You contain all the ridges and ranges foolishly
conquered, valleys and canyons tramped
and lost in shadow, because to you
pride and pity are equally absurd.

TICKET OF LEAVE

Home by the sea in a forest of towers
Black Prados growl the humid sky
Chase tickets to the tallest tower in the world
By a Persian raised in the shadow of Babylon
Until another topped his futility in my tourist
Town the towers are occupied by heathens
Closer to Heaven and without care any God
For what it's worth and nature are meaningless
To them they ignore the waves rising at their feet
At the top dive bar or ersatz thrill in harness
So I bought a ticket to the first unholy tower
Gone back to the big bang when
Noah's great grandson chose structure for agency

In the language of risk cash blows in the clouds
Absent above the sea they are bound immaculate
Without remorse sand secretly eating their toes
The lingua franca of slim plastic
On Kale Tuesday he leaned over and whispered
My work once more is done you cannot enter here
Those old days must be gone we made
Too much trouble for ourselves

Possibly the Old Testament decided I needed
Bringing down to Earth no surprise
Nimrod's castle in *The Tower of Babel* is smaller than me
Because scale and perspective are infinitely potent
Foremen and managers grimace in his shadow
What happened to the barge who does the hoist
Cook cries her mason is buried haulers and carvers
Hear me beg no favour still the sky does not open

Sipping wine the Calydonian Boar drips retribution
A minister sweats hard dodging rocks
Catapulted by rent seekers in harlequin suits
Payment made crouching on crags in dark waves
Head down his blind eye does not fear
The storm bringing destiny like Ouroboros
Turned around the Karnak obelisk pin stripe suit
Stiffened with gold lining heart encased in pitted
Lead he does not mind the noise because
Appeasement is more than another's reward
And to know power is not to understand how
An Austrian in the tower with a Korean phone
Makes bad sense to the maid without a passport

Moulding fruit of their labour sags
Scaffold holds foundation all the mechanics
To frame a jigsaw a noise to compete with
The coming noise toiling at the juncture of
Agriculture and industry on the drunken stairway
Engineering supersedes what passes for morality
Revealed as hubris or an elegant tactic so they
Do not deliver themselves but remain in awe
Receding like the horizon on a road trip
As death overtakes if they do not arrive
Their place will always be there

I was deep among them with Bruegel who wore their clothes
Beside *The Fight between Carnival and Lent* not taking sides
The melee wheeled I gave my silent looks to Spring Autumn
Winter so poignant it was visceral before the room began
To fill the mischievous ones from *Children's Games* spilled
Out of the frame crowded in the square in front of the tower
Waking from sedation like pets they entered this different plane

Ears wrapped in unscrambled tongues paying no attention
To no one explaining the fate of the world at the café I too
Licked ice cream until my ticket not wholly spent
Still a long way to go I struck out for the nowhere coast
Conscript tickets not transferable they remain
Trapped in the tower marked never to be released

ITALIAN JOURNEY

Rosaria, not Mr Google
We do not need language

Grattacieli e tunnel
New York 1930
Fortunato Depero
Offered the hearty food
He cooked in the afternoon
Even then no one came to see
His wonderful pictures
How sad that night the
Salsa di pomodoro

Rovereto's famous son
Passed the next twenty
Years making omaggio

Rosaria, put the phone down
Come to the window
Listen to the cellist
Heartbroken in the square

THE SIGNING

Her long curve
Leans into him straight up

Trunk a silver silken gown
The train of buttress roots

Surrounds his soft suede long coat
Brown like volcanic loam patched with

Leather fringes and bark stuffed pockets
Waltzing at their wedding

Long gone still the music plays
We notice a bare section

Bleached grey at the top
Saloon keeper and his sweetheart

Gone rogue this elegant couple
Touched by a white finger

One in a million they looked at us
Bowing witness to them

Our light shines still
We are blessed again

GINA

An earnest young man climbs a ladder
Hanging lanterns on a branch or placing
Bottles of high potency on a shelf.
An older woman signals to him
From the lounge. I ask, what are you doing?
She replies, I was married under these trees
The light is falling, soon she will be here.

ARMS CONTROL

Imagine every American
Wanting a gun

Required to fight
Duke it out in the ring

By lot men and women
Winners awarded a licence

For one year
Imagine the shame

VENICE

I drift in low among the reeds
Anchor behind this ageless tide
To weigh the scene discreetly
My eyeglass fills with countless
Sozzled somnambulists
Rolling around the Ducale

Adding to the pock marked
Scrawl of mould misty veiled
Sulfur light all shimmy and quiver
The curve of the prow scoops
The towering hull yesterday
Ground into the wharf

Circumspect of Bogarde on the Lido
I could turn a page of Marco Polo
Listen to waiters blow smoke
In the piquant back alleys
Plotting against superannuants
Never so sure empires will fall

In the Danieli wistful statues
Anticipate the Doge's call
Fossicking Canaletto postcards
Masked already for tonight's ball
No way my Murano paperweight
Displaces all that surface tension

PERCEPTION

I look down into the creek and see the smallest leaves
Ten times as high so close they could tickle my palm
If I could leap without falling without leaving the ground

I have walked far what I recognise now has been visible
All the way an inverted image flipped beyond the focal
Point trembled doubly by water as well as wind

I try to imagine William Robinson recognising inversion
As method but I see it as message the flipside of each other
How prescient the creek reveals we are not different

THE KELPEELER

One half chest blue the other red alternate socks
The kelpie cattle dog arrives eagerly ahead of me
At the crest of the hill and stops bat ears and wolf tail erect
Something is up a brisk wind ruffles the tail's thick hair
Caressed in rhythm with vivid green blades of grass
She peers into a dark domain of sprawling fig trees
Taking stock of the sub tropic Queensland tableau
Crowned with an orange halo growing by the second
Cushioned by smoke conjured by a stage magician fierce
As approaching death wrapped in shining clouds bulbous
Like mutated pearls unmoved she processes the fury sniffing
At the trees the clouds flame alight as I appear tumultuous
Red parachutes rearing up and out every way
I turn tail in light rain and stealth back down the hill
Harlequin races ahead circles around plants legs apart
Head tilted brow furrowed fixes me with her stare
We breathe together and wait while the sun sets

1981

You see, nothing is real anymore. Such timing. The night of the Oscars is when he dies. He said we have every right to dream heroic dreams. Young Hinckley and his dream. He gave it to Jodi who has to live with it and Mrs Brady and Nancy, but none of them want these dreams. It is the weight of dreams. He quotes WC Fields in speeches and grumbles 'oh damn' from the hospital bed. Okay, who'll be Vivien Leigh? Jodi? Rhett Hinckley Jr could be Ashley who is Dr Spock who is Darth Vader who is Redford who is Roger Moore with Olivia de Havilland who is Hepburn who recognised De Niro who is Captain America who might have been him if he wasn't Nixon first and certainly isn't James Brady. If facts don't lie. Which is better than no facts at all. The first day of April. He will never die. He will eat 1984, Blondie and Bowie for breakfast and then burp on Hinckley before sending Nancy to Vietnam and eloping with Jodi who didn't like the Red Square anyway. The Middle East will rust and Lech Walesa will suicide. The Ayatollah will be deposed. When is the real thing not the real thing? When nobody dies. Brezhnev takes hash oil intravenously and reads daily horoscopes. The Iron Maiden is Helmut Schmidt's fish wife. De Niro has cauliflower ears. Mao is alive and well and renting rooms off Idi Amin. According to the *San Francisco Examiner*, in Tulsa, Oklahoma, English was the last class of the day for seventh graders at Tulsa Central Academy. Just before dismissal, the principal came on the intercom and told them he had been shot. About ten students began cheering. There is a definite possibility I will be killed. It is for this very reason that I am writing you this letter now. As you well know, I love you very much.

PATIENT CHART

Hair plastered back, wet reeds on the sand at low tide
Moustache string a moment when scribbly gum found its line
You let your face shine, wide lapels, gleaming black shoes
Always on the Flemington favourite, after the sanatorium
Whatever the odds, you wore tuberculosis with honour

White lab coat hovers low in the white sky
Never quite the stiff blanket before voltage tried
To stand you up for your crimes, you remained
Laid low, the Bayerischer Wald sparkling out of reach
Your shame dulled head turned away

No one wears submission anymore for better
Or worse, memory serves like press ganged navvies
We are sentenced for the blue whale, the bilby
Their gaze never infectious, nothing to prove
They have no mercy

NATURE STRIP

The one we call Yeah Nah with hair like white snakes of Medusa

The one who keeps chickens and says we are twelve here

The one whose son is called Carlton

The one who uses ice and parks facing the wrong way

The one who sold us a filing cabinet we wheeled down the road on a trolley

The one who bought the house because it looked like the seventies

The one who borrowed to build a deck and lost his job

The one who leaves out traffic cones labelled "drive carefully children
        playing"

The one whose swimming pool has a pair of leaping dolphins in the tiles

The one who paid over the money because he wanted to live in Benny's
        house

The one barred from the letters pages of every newspaper

The one whose wandering wife was found at the airport

The one who spies the choppers and the children perched on the roof

SANDSTONE CAVES

We rumble the turnoff
Quieting wood song on stone
Pick Hardenbergia sprigs
Purple haze to hang
On the rear view mirror

Empty face staring she
Swivels tack waiting
Out of frame a sphinx looks
Up two steps more a Monaro
In the backyard familial

Alcoves contain only absence
Carved with emu feet walls of
Swirling rain pastel smoke
Faint whispers behind open
Windows on outstretched arms

Framed by spindly trusses holding
Bluest sky sharing Uncle's
Laminated face incongruous
The only one who shows himself
A ghost or a song we might sing

For ersatz seekers in urban black
Scrambling inside digging footprints
In this sacred dust they say
Well others were here

She turns on her long legs
Faces the heat frozen crest
Marathoners straggling behind
Slowly drink in the clouds

I wait in the wave face shadow
Struggle to reconcile for we
Cannot unhang the purple haze
What's done has left these
Afterimages of illuminance

ACTOR NETWORK THEORY

We gather every day
Always here at your place
Drifters and seekers
Never turning away
You rally and affirm
Magnet and beacon
Sustained by light that falls
Shaking and dancing
At your feet across
Our arms and legs
Painted in your troupe

You bend so generous
Allowed the kelpie to show off
Her motor skills ascending
Your shoulder like the
Bungarra whose skill
Ran like a current
Up to my head for a moment
Davy Crockett's hat

Do you remember the
Purple lotus passing through
She posed for an hour or two
Impressionistic gesture
On your lavender shag
The reverent father with
Two small children bearing
Everlasting tablets for you
To hold and give to others

I always stand back in this
Sensitised circus no cages
Whips or poles I wonder if
The chorus of tightrope walkers
Rehearsing off with your cousins
Their black box stuck on
Nothing but empty
Rhythms of repeat
Ever made the bright lights

We have no need of speech
For our gentle show
You director and architecture
We miming players gone home
When you take the bows
In the dark such is
The nature of our friendship

LEAVING THE GARDEN

My skin wrinkles with the bark I have planted not in seven days
Or even seven years what it takes to create a garden world
I can do less am needed less yet without me the garden
Is less alive I stand and hose rushing and howling
Like blood an extension of my arteries trees my limbs
My feet drink the clouds when it rains I am condoned
When I go I cannot leave fill plastic pots with pups chipped
Into new families they trail along dutiful exuberant prosper or fade
Unwild and reconciled to a forever child's fate
At the mercy of my hand I have made a sunken
Lounge where I have laid face down craving the grass
Gulping air to regain equilibrium skirted and tossed cane toads
Danced and sung and swam fired champagne cork cuttings
Reimagining weekends amid palm seeds an exploded solar system
Across the Buffalo Way by those rooted and then removed
Were they replanted elsewhere they would create their own
Dimension but as discards they exist in the abstract last night
I slept on the grass dreaming lost trees carried by fruit bats

PEAK BURLEIGH

At dusk the rainbow lorikeet chorus
doesn't miss tasselled rivals in the boho flock
reeking coconut oil hair like treacle
preening as dropouts their parents might have been
counterculture now in coffee queues sanctified on Instagram
prancing like flamingos in nude active wear waving plastic coated
cardboard cups at beefcake pelicans wrapped in flesh eating tee shirts
constipating shorts doing the strut on chicken legs
genuflecting to flightless goons guarding the rooftop bar once
a pond for fledglings displaced by pill pecking roosters
flicking butts at the Chinese restaurant cranes in the ancient lake
replaced by a Chinese tower soaring above the old theatre arcade
all the lights off but the lorikeets cannot be dimmed.
Michael Peterson's freak out mural finally makes sense.
It's almost all gone except in the barrel blanking out the crowd
this Burleigh peak rising like Liberace at the golden piano
dead white parrot on his shoulder.

THE GIFT

Falling like butterfly wings
On an angel waltzing

A bright window
Into the azure

Foiled like a sultan's slipper
Rails like the underside of a breast

Fin true and pure as a dolphin
Asking only to be trimmed

Riders of it excelled
No take off impossible

No manoeuvre out of reach
Picked up by the retired engineer

Passed to the artisan carpenter
The freelance designer

The apprentice renderer
Until on the drumbeat of miracles

It disappeared stolen into the lab
Given to analysis

Investors ruined by failed knock offs
The riders stormed the lab took it

Back argued over sharing
Cliques faced off it was hidden

In a cave a long flat spell
To reflect in anticipation

The next rider chosen by ballot
When the day came and the waves

Again rose up to the sky
The cave of course opened

It was empty
They crawled in
Destroying the impression

NERANG RIVER

Three days west at dawn
the ancient brown snake delivers

slow poison to Bosun's Landing.
One sip sends me to Harper's Wharf

distilled into pain made exquisite.
I watch blue singlet speculators

ruffle feathers of black swans
jam stolen cargo on log rafts

felled rolled dragged behind mist
cradling razor leaves.

Grinning ghosts of cedar traders
whistle faint tunes brittle

as moth wings spun into glass
robes floating all the way to the sea.

Ensign stuck they push on
wet stench lifting mouldy decks

crossing under a jaundiced sun.
Slow below sky's bed warps

the hand convulsing a wooden bridge
in the obsidian mountain shadow.

Sealskin girls on the far bank
dive for oysters tubby

like jewelled babies
until canals widen the loom.

Burgundy toads puff on a silver wharf.
A raft pulls up exchanges quick and silent.

I find Maqroll on the rocks
whales winking in your afternoon bliss.

JETSKI CADENZA

Wind above current below
Brushing down ploughing up

Sublime time parsing visibly
Wings open lifting

Random morning song
As they saw the dinosaur

An orchestra warming up
My feet touch the edge

Not that same water
The same old place

Slowness draws me closer
A participant in hope

Become anticipation
Now you are here

Cranky snarling stupid
Horns encased in rubber

You pass the crossroad
Hacking in the front row

Until strings and wind
Resume in good time

ARGOS IN ASHMORE

Argos sat by the feet of Telemachus, staring at the spaces between the leaves. Telemachus was shining the head of a spear and softly reciting a poem he had made about Argos. Together they glanced now and then at the river in the gloaming.

Telemachus failed to notice Zeus so faint behind the dark clouds only Argos could hear. When Telemachus looked over again to admire the copper river he saw Argos had disappeared, absent from the moment when the thunder grew loud.

Telemachus went to the gate he had carelessly left open. Rain began to fall. Grevillea blossoms in the yard caught the limpid light shining like the coloured beacons in the Polis harbour.

Argos was roused by a warning of violence and doom, of the sky crashing the palace, drowning the forest scents, filling the nymphs' cave, routing the trails. He ran to escape the end of the world.

Telemachus walked to the street, calling out for Argos but only the neighbours were summoned, shaking heads, shrugging shoulders. Telemachus' throat went dry when his mother Penelope appeared, adjusting her gown. She asked him why he was shouting. He could not speak except to say the dog's name. Lightning lit up their faces. The thunder roared and crashed.

Argos ran on the highway beside cars and trucks, weapons he could not recognise because his fear of thunder was greater, until he was hit by a river whiff. He aimed for the riverbank and the rocks and the water. The highway traffic screeched like startled cockatoos.

Argos stood shivering behind buttress roots of trees great as contented
Polynesian kings and queens. He watched the rain and the river
become one, drinking in the smell of stirred up waste and decay. He
heard voices of the ancestors and saw his master at last, in battle.
Argos lifted his head opening the white fur on his throat and yowled a
long contrapuntal note to the thunder's bass.

A young couple saw the dog by the river in the storm and they knew he
was lost. They spoke to Argos and the ancestors' spell was broken.
They invited Argos into their car. He was photographed panting on the
back seat, pink tongue lolling. Around the neck of Argos, the young
couple found a bone tag with a phone number.

Later in the night, after the thunder retreated, Argos returned home.
Penelope fell to her knees and embraced him. The young couple
watching drew closer to each other in moonlight blurred by the rain.

Telemachus returned to his poem in which Argos became a beloved
hero. Argos was not changed. He would always fear thunder.

DOMESTICATED ICONOGRAPHY

Alone with Jose Lopez Portillo
The President of Mexico
We had nothing to say
Respecting the silence
Of the wheatfields
Obedient stalks
Drinking down
A belting sun
Only they could pierce

Abducted smuggled hung
Here above me
Sentenced to this lonely hot house
In another dry world

At midday I left Portillo
To keep my hallucinations company
Drove to catch a breeze
At the ugly rock fringed
By offerings of plastic scrap
Chorus of flies at the drum
I scrambled to the top
Searched for the sea
Beyond the silo
Where I might not swim

In the evening I sipped cheap shiraz
Slurped canned bolognaise
Portillo graciously demurred
Listened as I reminisced
Gazpacho with Stalin in Kreuzberg

Mapo tofu with Mao in Shanghai
By most accounts not entirely innocent
Portillo was uneasy in such company
The benevolent gaze of the damned

Relieving for *The Advertiser*
All summer a perverse echo geopolitical
Soft power at vacated Northam
I wished for sultry Tretchikoffs
Dreamed only once that slow moment
Jesse James nailing a picture to the wall

KOALA

The truth is not yet fire
Even as it licks our faces
Your ghost face penumbra
Our fingers desire
Your black spot curse
Stoic old mussel wearing
Silver beard wire
Your frown of helpless disgust
Unstitched eyes
Weeping the puss of horror
Your infected children chewing

Faeces wet bottom dirty
Tail marks trivialised for wild
Dogs and cats the gun the knife
Because you were soft
Oklahoma to Oslo
Cuddling our sanctified pyre
You cling in stolen corridors
Cut chiffonade by subdivider
Artisans of natural selection
We may as well bid you gone
For all our hand wringing

HARD CURRENCY

An escaped prisoner on a beach of jewels
Suspects perfection in abundance is worthless
So I look for the damaged and the miscast
Among these cast away houses of the dead
Smoothed in rocky baths of foam and salt

A bride weighed in mermaid brooches
Malabar cowrie and wampum strings
The Bornu King's revenue paid by every man
Flicked into money by the calligraphy brush
Sewn into Solomons cloth exchanged for kina

All this wealth minted in waves
Measured on the tide
An economy underfoot
Whorled pure under clear eyed sky
Enabled agency circumscribed
By attention to place
Until outstripped by white desire
Outlawed by silver and gold

A flint eyed miner made twitchy
By the fossil exchange
Might say the floating hoard
Is given up freely
If shells were money
After fire and flood
Beachcombers could be wolves
So I tell no one

PELICANS

Caribou DHC-4   incoming
In still air   elegance
Becomes you   we've landed

Barge arse backs up   smoko
Hey Jack   got a durry?
Strut   look around

Unfenced   level block
All sand   floods every day
By the concrete bridge

Flat circle   no cooking here
Our salty selection
We are boss   big mouth

Sharp smile   tip the cap
Laughing   cargo load
Watch 'em wriggle   goin' south

Burp   scratch   flash a wink
Hey Bob   can't say I do
How 'bout a prawn cocktail?

EELS

Nearing another beachcomber
Our arcs meeting in the tail
Of a storm mine ambling slender
His more urgent tighter older
He wore a wild fleece unruly hair
That south coast look men of a certain age
Display a sign perhaps of shared values
He reveals he is hunting eels
To eat from a swamp running a stream
Chasing out to waves shooshing
Drawing up but not touching
Parabolas destined not to meet
The stream spent across the sand
Greeting shells buoyed by a notion
Of eels strands of an advancing net
We scan the wet grains as dreams
Become possibilities a vision writhing
Out of distant time I waited for him
To lie down fine in his waving fleece
The moon cast a line across the sky before
He was soon enough wrapped in eels

AT THE BRIDGE

We slow down settle in
Front row seat, the open sky
Obviously, it's seen better days
Still, plovers flash in the wings
Humpbacks squash the stalls
Sea eagles own the rafters
No one disappointed
The soundtrack is off key
Fats Waller in his cups
More fractured wind chime
Than shiny baby grand
Any way you listen
The melody is worn loose
Rhythm boggy as wet sand
Soft under stout wood
Deep cracked and tilted
Holding up, that's the charm
Smile now wave a small
Blessing, it's my turn to roll
Begin my Cuttagee sonata

HAYWARDS BEACH

All that is known and all that ever was.
They contain these finite things. And more.
Secrets stacked beyond literate,
fissures of code bending the unbendable,
the mantra of hissing light as spirits.
Too easy to say one is him, the other her.
Where I stand blind in the liminal zone,
meeting the past, rolling back my aesthesis,
architecture is unmade,
icons invisible to ideologues,
I feel lava chills, rough fur of salt,
the rhythm of rippling plates,
cool eruptions of Artemis.
Others grow weak but not these,
their fount is deep, locked in folds,
horizons shimmied and rolled,
inexorable wholeness and harmony.

ELEGANT CUNJEVOIS

The tide has fallen around this sessile colony,
old grey pot stickers clung on rocks, tough
leather tunics of cellulose polysaccharide
draped in green sea lettuce. Their tunicate flesh
contains vanadium and lithium. They squirt,
we are ascidians, the ancient ones, we anoint
you with this sea, this holy sea blood.
I reply, amen, holy cunji, amen.

Darwin suggested ascidians and vertebrates diverged
at an *extremely remote period* among those first
to recognise self from non-self here brainless yet
managing to avoid taxes, mortgages, school fees.

Tide rising strokes the preening pack
filtering oxygen and phytoplankton, pharynx
filling the pharyngeal basket. Spawn arrive and depart
twin siphoned termini, testes and ovaries ticking
together to different tocks. Larvae with hollow
notochords silent hunt one of their own or a rock
to head stand. Twin glands on the head secrete cement.
Hermaphrodite grips, I absorb my tail, my recycled
brain becomes a ganglion, I complete me.
Natural transubstantiation, neither Xenomorph nor
Mugwump, washed up like puckered fingers.

In the clifftop mansion, wrinkled king, pearly
queen, iron gates festooned with rusty bicycle parts
shape shifted into twirling flowers, twisted skinks,
beaming suns, those dudes stare down at the dog
picking 80 per cent human DNA.

OLD HORSES

We are spun out around you,
arms elbows hips a reclining curve
in the merciful hills of a country town,
below the coral tree, soft edge on the sky,
mooching at the blessed cone, coloured
glass winking in a wondered shack.
Always you are the first I see, sipping coffee
at dawn on the quarterdeck, together unhitched
from your carousel, humble as dry grass.
Modigliani's awkward coquette, a long centre part,
body sculptor veins on bulging flanks, ignoring
the crumbled planks at the fallow door,
spanning continents, wings folded, barely moving.

Rising from the shallows not five clicks from here a rocky head,
four hundred parsecs out there a star forming nebula,
I suspect you walked the coast road for the cup. Not now,
the bolts are stowed, apocalypse not our gig, carrying
no one, slow step nodding to silent glories in languid time.
We float by like enchanted equestrians
dancing the Grecian bend in a ghostly zoetrope,
exquisite balm of a string vibrating to the slide.
We don't mind you grinning in our face.
The head on the rock is lowered,
the stars, the stars are young.

OYSTERCATCHERS

After EAP

Lamp left glowing shelves untended
out from dust whispering in the attic
picking a path to the windy jump off.

Hooded messengers delicate black
on wet spikes wings rampant they foil
shoots and sparks like shiny magicians.

Lethal quills dipped in damp stratus
stained red a warning surely heeded
patient for the lull each red eye clear.

Do the bloodless in shadows below
sigh again for that sudden reprieve
written on wind in the swoop away
their desperate fate to wait evermore?

These hours are not strained by lonely
nights no tapping at the window it is
the gush and rumble of fearless waves.

POET'S HOUSE, BARRAGA BAY

For Rodney Hall

There is no house
the house is gone
burned inside out
his word wake blinking
under a jumble leaf sky

Reason stands off feelings
echo faint stanzas in the scrub
pathos smokes like pollen
misfortune becomes productive

Morning pastels blue and green
caress the smuggled cove
dreams from the amber creek
enter vanished rooms of consequence

Kelp fingers whisper open forms
in submerged caverns
a house being absent
might then float on a tide song

Crumbled bush rock wall
guards the ring unlocking
language of unseen birds
do not forget the cry of gulls

Demosthenes in forest shade
half shaven pebbles in his mouth
turns and bows tangled declamations

A ruin might reveal evidence
the embossed bottle clay pipe
white powder in a cloisonne pill box
make scattered ghosts come alive

You are like the unbreaking wave
sanctified presence invisible
what's unwritten is unfinished

When the bough breaks it brushes
her shoulder terrified she jumps up
vanishes into silence

BLACK SWAN LAKE

The last black swan in that urban lake
Others at the cedar table call a borrow pit
Resulting from excavation to make up ground elsewhere
Outside the limits of construction
Required to be reclaimed as if the predator can make good his prey
As if an implied promise accepts the return may be not postponed
In which the borrow is perfunctory without compassion or regard
Recognising this black swan dying before time nonetheless
As anticipated is failing to adapt rather than failing to live
As if failure is disappearance

An unpredictable event with potentially severe consequences
Based on the assumption of non-existence
In which disbelief hatched a wondrous adynaton
Measuring impossibility before de Vlamingh lifted the gaze
On that nobility of the curved neck of couples
Ballroom dancing on the *Swarte Swaane Drift*
Taken by Baudin to Josephine's menagerie
Conveniently decried a witches' familiar
To bake a swan scald it and take out the bones

A vision then of black swans appropriate even further south
In this tidal lake gravitating with sand rather than resentment
Extending heads below bodies in the causeway lee
Across diminishing shallows engineered to progress
As if dominance presupposes eternity is inconceivable
To all but a few and the path that blocks is the right path
As if the limits of construction are not barbarous
The return to non-existence not imagined
Waiting for the cauldron to fill with sand

GOING VERTICAL

After the end of innocence
widow maker went vertical,
watch him bury a rail,
foot down on the bend.
I go up for the ride,
pink fluoro to black sleeve,
dropped arms in the pit,
gunfighter striding out
from a fireball screen.
Don't look back, it's luxury
to commit mayhem.
The wave is clay turning on
a wheel. Eyeball counters
losing their way once
were outlaws. Always
somewhere a gull is dropping,
head down, wings pinned back.

THE LINE, GULAGA

Yuin Country
with respect

Making a spell of irresistible grace
the mountain line unwinds
like a high cast unfurling
gentle pull of the moon

the line disrobes
at a tempting beach inaccessible
like a catwalk curling around
an equine silhouette unridden
fierce as forever in a mirror
blinking backstage

they come walking for the silhouette
the pedant catalogues light
angles shadow at the high
place long exposure of the oldest pose
comforting because it is unachievable

others shoot themselves on the line
love before the silhouette
upswells after the click
the lost child asks
there you are she says
they regather lock arms
turn to face the line and in low
voices say what they see

stopping at the line knowing
the time taken and given up
to remain the old couple
smile thinking what they see
affirms their completeness

the oracle at the tip receiving sacrament
remarks offhand if you want a water view
turn on the tap how it began in the rain

I walk the estuary to the oval arrive
at the bar where the mountain is most
exquisite and follow the line back to remember

NAMING MT DROMEDARY

Fooled again this time
Hicks found Cape Flyaway,
fog cloud on the sea,
peering bent in the wind.

For the next pages coat
buttoned inking rocks,
enough lustre for the peers,
nearest I might be to the King.
To call a mountain a camel
the mountain made me smile,
dubbing for a while was not a chore.
I was again pleased with myself
not bringing the kind of distinction
of worthy image making.

On the beach another camel
in the rocks gazed resolute.
From the mountain
they saw a pelican,
made smoke into story.

SAM SINCLAIR

How fires the soul of a town if the luminary is a smithy and a saint?
Hammering sense into object: what kind of philosopher does that?
Is this what Prometheus had in mind? Boer War farrier on a bicycle,
Grafton to Bermagui, pocket shillings miniatures of muscle.
Tools from his taffy made fish dancers in the Kings Hall,
alchemy right there at the forge on Horseshoe Bay.

To cool down the wheelwright weighmaster strung up, hung not
hanged, big bill trophies snapped like Joe Byrne without
contortion, smooth bellies of brushed metal.

Sledgehammers broke rocks on his dray builder chest. Arise
from the clay furnace, teeth puller made Don Athaldo,
world's strongest man, fostered the Down child Violet with Lily:
the temperature of perfection is not strained.

They signed his form, heavy apron in all the pubs,
'Here's Too'ee' at Central Station, daily balm for the desperate
quietly banging carriage doors. When the horse slowed coffin
maker built the service station, taxied from the wharf, marvel
chugging in a Minerva, sharp exhaust floating with steam
in the clear eye of Gulaga.

His cottage, pitched roof, ragged sail until the sale notice
appeared. Give us your home, we turn it into easy money,
we of the flash beard, winklepicker soles. No effort.
He was their beacon, they glowed in his spark
until he fell from a ladder unburned.

MADE HEAVY

She arrived late, carried by the flood on a broken raft,
discretion unforeseen, beauty unformed, still unknown.
Drifted in the leaves waving on the edge,
settled her gaze, turned away the glory of the water
like black polished stone because she
will not look into the eyes of the mountain.
Night passed. She raised the sun in her
hands. Across the sheen bronze glow not yet ripe
to rise and fall shimmered in the trees, a bright
murmuration. I can rise beyond being here
if I step into the lagoon, sink my head, and breathe.
She smiled at me in the soft light of cool
hands poured into fire. From this day forward
she was made heavy. And I the possessed.

SHOREBREAK

Cymbal, drum, trumpet, cue
juggling knives on a unicycle,
vanishing as you crash.
We remembered the last,
cheered for the next goal
celebration of Neptune's
vaudevillian. Until you began
to creep forward, met the stalls,
broke the fourth wall, took us
down on puffy knees, calling
in our debt payable to the sky.
Behind the curtain, backstage,
I'm ready again. Boardies,
tails, bowler hat. I grin at them
gasping as I go down.
Kamehameha on the tiki bar.
Velvet shade with tassels.
Ship's clock a wheel stuck
on midnight. You spit banksia
serrata's golden inflorescence.
I walk out a witness on the surge.

VESSEL

It followed me like a ghost
And now at last I grasp

Like the beatnik monk
He was wrapped up in it

The boy in the tree alone
Knowing joy in melancholy

Something more ineffable
Taking with him the sweet pine

Scent of a young cone smooth
Unopened the first prickles

Tickling his palm in the plaintive
Well of late afternoon the first

Message of time slowed down
She found for him the Buddha

Rubbed smooth in Beijing dust
Fingers wrapping a mahogany base

A red flagon from the Bay factory
Dug out of a Berlin bunker borne

Unbroken like an icon in procession
Like the burning bush in my hand

CAFÉ HACKER

Early, after dawn, south coast New South Wales, sun
pooling in the wave lights the way. Four in a set slide
down the bank, crystal runners peaking off the final turn.
On the lookout bench, a Café Hacker cup lost in shadow,
too late for the nomad gone. Mozart's silhouette transfer
doesn't blink at the time signature on the shore.

Ninety minutes from the Bavarian border, Rattenberg,
Sudtiroler Strasse 46. Midday coffee drinkers frown
in winter lamplight, respite from the glass angel factories.
The mountain shadow runs four months, anneals into
seasonal affective disorder, tiredness, a feeling of being
good for nothing. I can see the sun across the river
but cannot feel it, the cake in front of me but cannot eat it.

Burgermeister's heliostat would pass the sun like a baton.
Glass always saved the old duty post. We can run down
the clock. Gloom prevails. Souls are warmed by gold leaf
saints in Virgil's kirche. They pray to Mary in the grotto.
Mirrors shall not change the long turn of forsworn light.

AFTER MIDNIGHT

You can see him in the top corner,
overpainted chiaroscuro gone smoky.
Pillbox hat, silk cravat
laid on the last church pew,
Dylan drilling in the wall.

Euclid the card table lookout
with the brocade gamblers
and the bunny girls, a confident
smile, he's done the numbers.

Jack Johnson on the bandstand
teaches Tommy Burns jazz on a cello.
Spinoza crouching at their feet
spies a crucifix on the tuning peg.

Aristophanes at the bar tells
the blind sheriff and the pock marked
priest how the Russians eat caviar.

Jake Gittes grins in the swing doors,
too late for sweet Marie, she's out of
frame trailing burgundy velvet skirt.

In the safe, the gangster found a small
Vermeer stolen by the Nazis. Desdemona
sold it for cash in a suitcase, took a train
with Peter Lorre to the end of the line,
missile fair at the Polish border.

TRAWLERMAN

Take this cold capstan
bleeding rope fingers
white rubber boot of
old rusty tail yellowfin
lead reel trailing cumulus
guts on skinned decks
of flathead eyes smearing
iridescence this gimlet
fouled octopus this cuttle
clung to mackerel stern
in snapper latitudes of
beatific bream taste this
ling slipped up from my
oeosphagus ululating in
my flaxen gills tally my
plight on the black pearl tray
mark my slick throw me back
every blood moon as I wander
in heaving circles never
seeing my disappearing love
until she dies at my feet

THE GALLERY, ALBURY

One took my money, the other my coat.
Both had gaps in their front teeth,
gaps of possibility. She told me to open
the small doors, look for the broken pieces
of the found made whole, wait on a Sunday
in winter in the pine forest.
I opened a white door, took a long look,
saw them lie down in the needles.
She laid her head on her sister's shoulder.
Trees dotted the wall dense after the hailstorm
killed the Tingari at Lake MacDonald.

EISBACH

When I was done you had only begun,
knowing each wave might be your last.
Every wave you rode was my lost wave,
another of the thousands I had to let go.
A party wave, your crew queued
like seals holding joy sticks
waiting in the park, in the city,
under the trees, in the cold, your turn
daring to dance or take a beating.
I saw the wave as your minute hand,
striking not sand but cement, a long plank,
skein of rope, endlessly running
over, never spent day and night,
no genuflection to tide or wind or swell.
Your wave derived from melting ice
warmed your aching soul even as your light
dimmed. You showed me the moves
I knew like my heartbeat. I tried to
forget that part of me gone in the breath
of every wave. You made me remember
my waves, watching you claim
another and another, slim, elegant,
minimal, generous in your dismount for
the next rider, surely not me. I am grateful
you showed me what I could no longer do.
Your wave continues as you are gone,
my wave gone, still I am here, both of us
unbroken in ways our waves will never be.
You chose the wave to ride out,
the wave replays your ride,
your close out our great loss.

BLACK STUMP

Did not even turn the other cheek
When the Devil came with his red whips
Peeling bark like skin torn to make eagles
Cry above black Venus arms
Lost where greed has broken spoil
To call them headless martyrs
Insults their dignity who among us
Would die and stand so tall
In a brown paddock of cold wind

VELVETS, THE NULLARBOR

Black angels rise from hunks of tread,
soar and swoop over crazy skid marks,
pick harmony from belly-up lizards,
flyblown roos, blood shiny, skin like hard
leather, haunted by the refrain of Sunday morning.
Bitumen's theatre of violence. Gaunt trees
do the twist with spinifex, expressionless.
White stone, yellow stone, orange stone,
unmarked cairns, wrecked stubbies,
red dirt, dust and scrub huddles.
Eternity passes in each slow beat.
Emptiness filled with screaming viola.

DALI'S AMERICA

Perambulating on Geary Street,
pulled up by a Dali in the window,
grotesque stick like incarnations
I suspect Dali believed were beautiful.
I am convinced this callow day,
this Dali is America.
New York an organ not distinctly a heart,
cataclysmic conglomeration in torment.
Florida a drooping gland,
San Francisco a plumbing of pipes and taps,
a comb of golden blades in the centre.
Certain I am staring America in the face,
I ooze inside, tell the attendant sharp
in a dark pinstripe, I like the one in the window,
the one with the waggly tail.
He turns into a blank smile,
decides he does not agree, insists he cannot see.
Dali's America remains in the window
for another three days, on the fourth day,
Dali's America is taken away,
as Dali is turning into a snail,
paranoiac peacock eye
making place into space for a place of exchange.
I recognise at last on the page the unseen,
a face to perform arousal is not America,
nonetheless temptress, Man Ray's picture
of Duchamp's head, horns lathered in cream,
on bond notes with interest for believers
in winning at roulette,
makes space for Elon Musk to buy
comic sans Dogecoin on Binance.

ANOTHER REPORT

Another report by those scientists
Crunches the numbers contrary
The latest sly slant unwilling
To give up the dark shadow

Friends, you seek the truth
We can expose the scare
Tonight, the plain facts
Another report by those scientists

Coral bleaching's a touch of the sun
Common enough like sunburn
Our sponsored analysis never wrong
Crunches the numbers contrary

Emissions rise in limitless skies
Equate to healthy profits
Screams demanding action are
The latest sly slant unwilling

Coal miners all punch drunk
Retraining halts our progress
This is the price you pay
To give up the dark shadow

Too many agents of denial
Plot distraction from emergency
Ignore these rants call calmly for
Another report while the valley burns

THE LOWDOWN

'Possibilities discover
reality's shortcut:
The world arises.'
Signe Gjessing

Balloons are a fleeting divulgence of cheer.

Tacky pedestrianism is hopping molten sand.

Short haired cats with Big Macs and sax pack into jets.

Feverish gaiety craves aloof sophism.

Beauty tips give apparition luxury length.

The sneer on the pretty face is the cute mess around of the interpretation.

Etiquette is delightfully upset.

Infantile cruelty is disaster chortling with excitement.

The snarl of wildlife blows the ashes of fashion under the lights of ritual.

The ambition condition is ammunition, once somewhere never near enough.

Jingoism is the rapture of Movietone.

An assassin is only ever seen at a million frames a second.

A new government flies a sacred kite.

Booming silence is an aural vision of the distance of pitch.

A man in thongs is proud to be Australian.

Anxiety is fear of doubt and the spry absconder of hope.

Irony is the trick of triumph.

Sin is such a sweet little word, but dignity is silent.

The impulsive ferocity of the allegoric gesture is concealed within the subtle resonance of the turbulent rhythm.

A hard-earned thirst is the beginning and the end.

Infection is the only anarchy.

Only right and wrong are only prisoners of each lonely other.

Damnation is the eternal hurling of confusion.

The need to want is to wait.

The theatre of pressure is the storm of indecision generated by the mask of paranoia.

Infinity is the moment of falling asleep.

The pleasure of sacrifice is the scourge of restraint.

Credit prospers in proportion to the decline of trees.

Imagination is far too much to be science, but science is too heroic.

Eclecticism is the freedom to think rationally about an irrational arrangement.

There is surprise in calculation, calculation in surprise.

Exaltation is impulse without conflict.

The end of a dream is an intangible ageing.

The city simian evokes a sagacious crudity of candour.

Premonition is life in a day.

Being yourself is coming to your senses.

We just can't get enough of what it is we want.

TELL ME

Now that I have failed
fallen over failing
laid down and let failure fail all over me
waited for failure on the street in the rain
called out to failure in dark glasses and a wig
found failure in the passenger seat with a goofy grin
scrolling my phone
sat down with failure for wagyu eye fillet
Ottolenghi sweet potato and Rusty Fig Tempranillo
no split bill
sung to failure the song *Hidden Charms*
at someone else's party
given up on failure because failure gave up on me
tell me about failure

HANG TIME

A heart floats soft
in pelagic sky

beating a blur takes guts
to remain up there

waiting out the wind
easier though if you are

but a skerrick
and you do this every day

ride the lift down
when the crosshairs line up

or do you play
like dolphins in a wave

catch and hold the breath
as you vanish back

into broken cloud never
the burden of endurance

DESPATCH

The Pacific Garbage Gyre is turned
by a single blue Pepsi screw top fixed
to the end of a mahogany walking stick
in the shape of Gandhi's left leg from the ruin
of the Taj Mahal after the Great Flood of '49.
The walking stick is stuck in meltdown goo
from the Minsk reactor capping the Eiffel Tower
which, despite privatisation, remains embedded
in the skull of the last wild giraffe standing on
Donald Trump's golden table, carved from
the single chestnut tree at Gilgamesh's grave,
teetering on the shoulders of the thousand eyed bull
whose flatulence finally made the great whale
roll over withholding all knowledge of empathy.
The rafts can carry no more. This I have found.
Oh, and flowers hang from the clouds like fruit.
Nothing further. I request I be returned home
on the next available mussel.

MINE WARDEN

Dancers lit up white
in a shade of flashing light
arms waving sway and beckon.

Mine Warden glides
their way at tango speed
stroking Wallaga Lake

like a Cuban heeled tease.
Light goes down in this bar
of the oyster sky floor sharp

with husk and rocky blade.
Band is diaphragm wind
hardwood percussion

urgent beat echoing above
the cry of stories
much the same fish

in the south always fish.
Ember smoke curls around
a sun burnished halo

on the warden's dark face
in an empty rum tumbler.
He pushes over his chair

rises with a rifle
to embrace the dancers
shake 'em on down

for they have drunk the poison.
Their fathers load gold
in the gentle dunes.

MIGALOO

Captain Chance called you his white blessing.
Breaching in the dark but not photographed,
did you still exist or take the longest taxi ride
to give birth, make payment
by staying alive?

We assume your ten times great grandfather
swallowed the prophet, bore the weight of our sins,
delivered doom on the day of atonement.
Those wicked would sacrifice all
after fasting and sackcloth.
The prophet became an agent
of resurrection or parody of disobedience.

I ran the deck to stay upright,
fled the head to meet the tail.
You showed your face, the room
swooned, our stare aiding extinction prevention,
or it hurt you, not too big to be the canary.
Have another beer, try the banana cake
muffled by engines in reverse.

To exempt justice, could you really bite
off a leg, or worse, fix obsession turned white
from staring into the black ocean,
praying you may return,
dragging us like a harpoon?

FLOWER DOME, SINGAPORE

When you live in the heat, you can rise on an air mattress.
The longer you live in the heat, the lighter your air mattress.
The higher you climb.
My heat limit is probably not yours.
We cannot all live in the heat.
Limits as a rule generally decrease.
My heat limit is dragons.
Lifted too high, dragon heat tightens my air mattress.
I can only slide off sideways.
No one projects heat like dragons.

Hydrangeas, agapanthus, delphiniums pose in blue gowns.
Bridesmaids safe on the floor of the cloud forest.
As I climb, I dodge somnambulating selfie sticks.
At the top of the cloud forest, a dragon fused to a tree.
Young women in black robes and mortar boards, laughing.
Unaware of the danger.
Starship Enterprise fills the windows.
A faint smell of sewage.
The Supertrees outside: ventilation shafts in disguise.

THE BULL AND THE OYSTER

Imperious as El Capitan
head turning slow as Mars
eyes marbled in the oldest quarries
always spent before he performs
convulsing on command
overcome by himself

Yes our eyes met across the Wapengo bridge
spanning his immense sadness
tempered by his great weight
no blame or choice but to accept
his line in the ledger
clock those beetles scuttling by his feet

I took the risk of reflected glory invited him
to swap tales forgave him my chair at the inlet
crushed while he sat like Solomon Burke
to forget for an hour his conjugal duties
offered him her hand in a wrinkled jewel box

She balanced trembling in his heart
until he placed her back upstream
folds stroked inside out
ripening like all the others while
he could only stare those marble eyes

POST OFFICE BLUES

The Orbost post office was finally demolished
to make way for a new replica post office.
It's the finally that grates and the make way
on the sign with a sepia photo like a lectern.

I should go home and return better dressed
if I am to enter the realm of the better parcel.
I am the lesser in the familiar,
the chipped crystal glass of port wine
on the cracked cedar chest beside
the cache of old letters loved and saved.

The Sale post office clock tower was bowled
over for a replica with the original mechanism.
Nothing final about the old clock
wound by timeless volunteers.
The dead letter tower delivers nothing,
the clock points to failure to admit regret.

They usually have reasons to disguise,
something to do with jobs and banks.
We know who they are, not here again
every day. Anyway, fewer letters come
and go, clouds disappear and reform.

WHITE DAHLIAS

Parade out from the tumble dryer
Persians   Turkish Angoras   Siamese
can-can dancing for weeks on end
until on necks the colour of absinthe
they turn pensive
models browning backstage
Les Demoiselles d'Avignon
smoking   sipping tea
picking hors d'oeuvres
with the orange and the lemon trees
so much flesh   what a sweet thrill
of the haunted   drunk and drawn
to their plush fingers

CORNFLOWERS

Queen Louise hid the children
in a field of sapphire braids
framing a well of conquered pride.

The scale of your beauty the essence
of longing for the infinite.

The children saved from Napoleon
they took you for the colour of Prussia.

You were cursed.

A badge worn by young men in silk in love
adding ecstasy to the palette
waving tortured from the mast.

The badge a portal to resistance
at the top of the stairs behind the iron door
knock twice and stand back.

You filled the eyes of stormtroopers
bayonets thrust you
into bloodstains above the heart.

CAMERA STUDIES

I.

The horses shuffle heads down in regret
for the mornings of mud and blood to come.
The party in silent black on carriages
stalking to the front
crosses a stone bridge in the mountains.
Shot from behind we cannot see their faces
only one has turned a hidden look
in shadow sly if not fearful
another walks in absent reverie.
The women under satin hats like shields.
The river charging white under the arch
so wide it howls
a Mahler symphony in high pomp.

II.

His world is small but contains everything.
A donkey a carriage framed by a stone gate
two mountains folded into the letter 'y'
the question neither asked
lit by a triangle of clear sky.
He stands attentive holding the reins
thick moustache straw hat
old suit with baggy knees.
She sits in high buttoned coat
mouth stern black hat wide as empire
without a thought for their absurdity.
Paused they stare at the one who takes aim.

We cannot see their eyes.
Order is preserved here before
another world wants answers.

III.

Farewell now in a dinghy
slow rolling on a glossed lake.
The two-stack steamer
resting like a dowager
asleep on a settee, soot and smoke
delivered up to an old muslin sky.
Mountains tumbling fathoms down
hold everything in place.
Those who led them with the horses to this shore
watch whispering in another language.
An old lady sits eyes down with two boys
swinging legs on a cart
beside a boarded-up warehouse
big enough to hide the weapons.
Unless this is not farewell but arrival.

IV.

My grandfather grew quiet behind his soft eyes
when he came home from the other side
of these melancholy pictures.
He helped others too door to door
all that needed doing
all he could do after the shelling stopped
and the bodies he no longer carried.

RESTRAINT

We stood in Vincent's room at the asylum
his bed, a chair, his portrait by another
a barred window, view across a lavender field
empty sky a disappointed blue.

Down the corridor a bathroom
two tubs covered with boards
only the head and feet allowed to extrude.
His first of eighty pictures here was *Irises*.

At Senanque Abbey it is said you will find
the perfect vision of lavender fields.
In the cloisters, an arch for each gospel
and within each, three arches for the apostles
scaled for the Golden Mean.

Every day, the monks are allowed an hour of talk
in a dark vaulted room, wooden chairs in a circle.
When they leave the room returning to silence
by a heavy door they are met by a stone head
painted red, the only bright colour on these walls.

After the death of Judas, Matthias was chosen
apostle by lottery, casting lots a convenient way
of resolving an impasse, what was cast is unknown.

Hordes engulf Senanque in buses
stomp the lavender fields
filtering perfection
ignore the modest signs
warning not to wander off the path.

HYDRANGEAS

Where I come from hydrangeas do not grow
in hot grey sand formerly mineral.
Where I am they glow
at Sarah's fence in quiet harmony
with fish. Her gift our duty to make gills
of turquoise, pink and blue.

Pitted by fire and salt, a cement pot,
rescued, I like to think, from a bush garden
almost entirely reclaimed above sand
so pure it sings and sparks
where a poet lived and if he stayed
almost died.

Black spurts formerly fish frames
dart past my shiny fingers
in their late summer,
settle into enjambment
ecstatic to fill the replanted pot.

Where I come from hydrangeas do not grow,
Sarah struggles with a hip stick,
the poet journeyed to where
hydrangeas exude gemutlichkeit
and we wait giving water
like oil lighting a lamp.

LEGITIMATE STAKEHOLDERS

Aiming for a heads up on the shitstorm
a reporter hurries across the square
"not boring" tattooed in Times New Roman
24 point caps on her small breast.
Balance a mirage, only a suite of voices will do.
She knows they want to and they will
because who speaks first has the last call.
Words become diamonds set in quote marks.
"The worst I've seen," he said, of course he did.
She knows that dirty old magistrate
naked on the ledge because she exposed him.
Two sharp pencils and an empty notebook
never fail. It's not rocket science but
a rocket scientist can't write the end
of the world in nine to eleven paras.
Anything else you want to say?

THE BALLAD OF HARRY BARRY

For I do not care for form
Care for form
Cannot care for form
Make form for form
Will not form from form
For care for make not form

For here we are, here we are, in fairest Tilba
Where, a long time ago, on fine autumn days like this
A most unusual event, a phenomenon, occurred, with a twist
To one Harry Barry, dairy farmer, Punkalla Tilba Road
Down by Victoria Creek

On Sunday, April 14, 1895, the sun hung in the sky like a promise
Milking done, Harry strolled out of the shed
For a puff on his pipe under the giant magnolia
On the way something, some movement
Caught his eye, the cows, a six pack, lined up on their back legs
Not fooling, dancing
Harry stood and stared, as you would
And then walked right at the apparition, until he could feel
The hot breath from their nostrils

Harry witnessed what might be recognised as clumsy, but sincere
Adaptations of the Watutsi, the Foxtrot, the Rhumba, the Cha Cha
The Hula and what appeared to be Gordon's Waltz, triggered in some
By excessive consumption of gin, although it might be said, these
Afflictions were not usually observed in cows

Dancing of course is a vigorous activity unexpected in cows
More likely to be unperturbed by an outbreak of dancing
In the top paddock, as might occur at Christmas or birthdays

Among the rocks, no, this was a frolic of cows without musical or
Vocal accompaniment, a puzzle to all but the most enlightened

Tors implacable guide all the stars
Under the pull of submerged fingers
An eternity of stories shape the hills
An inchoate gathering of minds
Aloof with condescension
Beyond the solstice
Because they may be more than gods

Harry looked into the cows' eyes and found, a twinkle of mischief
Or was that his reflected puddle of confusion
In any event, he saw an awakening, possibly even a pleading
Harry believed in miracles, so long as they gave cheer
But this vision, on this day, was, well, queer

Harry watched the dancing cows until he could stand no more
Sinking to his knees, he fainted
On awakening, salubrity regained, Harry ran back to the house
Wife Edith did not look up, from apples in the pot, stewing
Yes, Harry, I see, really now, can you pour the tea
The next day, Edith asked the vet, can you look at the cows

Picking tips on equatorial hills
Aching claws stiff as red hand on sore teat
Fill nests bound on bent backs
Slipping and falling, leech suckled, wasp and bee bitten
A million packs cargo stamped
A miracle unremarked by the steward blind also
To the crumpled flax puller of sail and suit
Harry and Edith sipped and gave thanks
As much as they knew in their own way

Safe to say Archie Cornish, the vet, had not yet encountered
Dancing cows in thirty years of animal ailments
Cornish attempted scientific diagnosis
The usual prodding and poking, cut short on this
Occasion by a sudden evacuation, as it were
Leaving him wet and sticky with the familiar stench
Of the veterinarian, so fruity it carried a warning
No dance partner required, was Archie's frank advice
More likely a human abnormality, an hallucination
Of proximity, best treated by a period of separation
Perhaps a lingering at The Drom, for two or three nights

The horseshoe above the bar, the wooden cross on
The altar pulse like dreams yet remain a mirage
The warm flesh, the sacred living, carries wonder
With ease, the seen chewing the unseen
Into essence, firing hearts imbued with magic
The same essence becomes hope or dancing
A pulse vibrating milk and all else to be imagined

Over the next week, evidently disturbing reports
Necessitated desultory investigation by John Cavendish
The Tilba constable, convinced it was another regrettable spree
Easily solved by dunking in the dam
Arriving sceptically at the Barry place, Cavendish observed
The bovine behaviour resembled disinterested somnambulists
Chewing steadily without moving any of their legs
Much at all, not even a sudden hop
Or run a few steps, only the sound of wind shaking the trees
And two kookaburras passing judgement
The innocent cows stared inscrutable at the copper
Nothing to see here
Cavendish made a note to switch his observation
To Harry Barry whose alarmist allegations were a threat to
Peace and good order

After the Constable turned his back, climbed into the saddle
And rode away, three of the girls threw their front legs
In the air and together performed perfect pirouettes round and round
Their great milk sacks like bloomers in the chorus line
At the *Moulin Rouge*, not that anyone had ever seen
Such a performance, until Harry Barry did

If order has moral value without impeachment
And if there is a season of liberation
How can that be everlasting without order
Unless order is suborned to allow
Release of the farmer kept by cows

Neighbours impatient, relatives worried, strangers puzzled
All were encouraged and cajoled by Harry through the winter months
To witness the miracle of the dancing cows
Nonetheless not one of those so invited observed, or suspected
Any trace of the fancy footwork spied alone by Harry
In his quieter moments

Harry was not an unreasonable man. As the weeks rolled on
Punctuated by high kicks, reels and jigs, and all the rest of it
Performed for an audience of one, Harry came round
To a realisation not realised before

To notice light flicking leaves into rhythm
To turn to face those leaves and unlock the gate
Shares relief to expand the known world
Makes the sun sing like Elvis
The moon swell the strings

By the spring, Harry had accepted the dancing was
A statement of claim, although why it was given to him
And no one else, he gave up trying to ascertain
I am alive, I feel pain, I seek joy, I want to be loved

Harry's sister, Clarice, asked, what poor brother has happened to you?
To which Harry replied, I have seen the ghost in the milk machine
And my gratitude hitherto exceeds my expectations

By the summer, milk from the Barry farm was known by a kind of
Euphoria, inducing in those who had most likely imbibed of it, a gait
Somewhat jaunty, and a habit to leave the paddock gates open

Gate (def.) 1. an opening permitting passage through an enclosure
Never looking back until under the magnolia tree they bend
And flourish a bough 2. a tower or architectural setting for
Defending or adorning an opening bowing to the arch
Bearing the words "for all our sakes" 3. Providing a monumental
Entrance framed by leaves each with a letter repeating
The word "respect" 4. an opening that leads to a place for boarding
Room enough to dance *Beat It* in the back alley
5. the total number of persons who pay admission of which
There may be only one and the price he pays is everlasting
6. the total receipts from such admissions counted in
Leaves of compassion 7. a channel or opening
In a mould through which molten metal is poured running
Into every vein along every crack that comes with
Perseverance 8. a signal making an electronic circuit operative
Or inoperative until release opens into a free festival of relief
Under black clouds on grass laid down with all this measured treading

FOR A BLACK BIRD

You're almost one of us
cushioned in sand

on your back in a velvet cloak
sugar pearl eyes turned away

in shame or pride
folded wings holding a memory

of the flight that made you free
strange you did not go up

one more time to drift
and stay beside the moon

I am your stranger staring down
at Rodin's *Monument to Balzac*

making them wait seven years
longer than you were alive

grotesque when revealed
hence the shame and pride

commingling as you toppled
to rest finally in the shade

where the maker waits unseen
knowing you only when you're gone

blessed to hold you in my gaze
given up when you did not rise

from above your wings out wide
cast this place tip to tip

PORTRAITS

Sun on the table at breakfast,
your buoyant smile adding warmth,
a portrait, *Munchener in Bermagui.*
Later, I admire you in the vegie patch
surveying the leaves of our content.

I was with de Chirico and his mannequins
lost in the shadows of Roman arcades,
until conjured together by jazz in old Shanghai,
they spied us beside the black balustrade
kissing halfway up the stairs.

We looked the part when the desk girl
unlocked that creaky room with the bay window
view of the Saone in Lyon, rode the funicular
to the basilica, stumbled on African blues
at the altar for the Sunday service,

found Cocteau's keeper in the fishermen's chapel
at Villefranche, pointing at Picasso drawn like a devil
under the cliffs crowned by a pink chateau,
the Ephrussi retreat from anti-Semites in Vienna.

A Georg Grosz horror show in the London gallery,
vile enchantment, staggering on crutches
so easily distracted by what they saw,
painted lips and nipples dipped in rouge,
only drew us closer together.

Had we become mere dilettantes
or perhaps artifacts
or the silver behind mirrors?

We landed in this spotted gum cathedral,
viewing from black duck latitudes
the death wish of a paranoid barbarian,
not simply by light from lithium and chips
but our complex candelabras of Angophora.

Riding the Sunova, now you are framed
hyper real, Teutonic warrior
dripping mercury on winged heels,
victorious smile enticing
the cold waves to draw breath.

SKUNKED

To set off from the Shell in the early quiet
ignoring my favourite rock the Camel
because anticipated wind holds
me in a roo's paws.

Hurtling past the cemetery where I go
to admire succulents on the artist's grave,
the house with 39 steps to enlightenment
(what were they thinking)
hunches back on the ocean. The islands

of the Three Brothers frown and the old lady
patrols the breeding birds with a lethal camera.
Bouncing over the bridge, a post
line of gaping mouths in heads
disembodied above the lake.

At the Murrah music hall, faded candy stripe corro
mulls over notes blowing leaves into treble clefs.
Clouds open pomegranate lemon
coconut, still too early to be safe.

Out of range, I tune whale song,
hover over the pedal to ride shooting stars
bouncing to Mimosa's vines peeping above
trellis until they're gone.

Down by the Balinese gods abandoned at the gate
to the beach of disputed ravines.
Suck rocks peep and rise peep and rise in

grey overcoats, not today. Swing by the cattle race
scaffold to eternity, not today.
Don't wake hidden sculptures cold
in spotty shade, please don't wake, not yet
deaf to my howling the whale song.
Another boomer explodes pinballing into
pittosporum. My console too hot to touch.

I'm on fire, brake in accelerate out
behind the dust screen. On the viewing platform,
the faces chop furrowed
worry lines whispering too late,
the wind escaped. If only we'd listened to

uncertainty of maps. We talk for a while,
ghosts in the banksia core sample,
but no one else is here.

BEN BOYD

Maneroo squatter swindles investors
Another colonial enterprise
Heathen cannibals
To fix the labour problem
Our man in New South Wales

You cannot defame the dead
These words lie
Unchained on the red rocks
Below your hideous tower

Others tried
Ben Boyd Road with a plaque
Boydtown subdivided
The Boyd Room at the Hotel Australasia
Still cold and cramped
Not a single bird in
Ben Boyd National Park
Has a good word to say

Your cargo bolted
Those words they signed
Only for you to libel them
Lost shepherds avoiding sheep

At your Seahorse Inn not a horse
To be seen or slandered
Deepest sea at Twofold Bay
Not enough to hide your guilt
To say nothing of the slaughtermen

Who climbed the tower
Cupped their mouths and called
A thousand whales

You might have tempted Kamehameha III
With all your sweet talk
Had the last word at Guadalcanal
When they took off your head

*Ben Boyd National Park was renamed Beowa National Park
in September 2022 after consultation with the Yuin people*

BUSHLARK

A song to carry close on your heart
a shield for one loving line

can shine or make a mark
wrapped in lasting step after step

the mark swift in softness or on stone
a ring or a beat to lift and steep

above not to roam or room but
to flourish or like home

written or stepped or doffed
shown or different grown

all over again or new or strange
a song to gift or meet alone

OLD COAL MINER

Old coal miner sways at the top of the stairs
Meat cuts swinging in a plastic bag
Opaque by his twisted leg
Calls out drunk across the road
I'm not going anywhere

It's not like he's never ridden a crusher
Never inhaled in Chennai
Coughing parts per million eyes wide open

Skin blotches cracked and torn
Blue and brown depressions
Dissolving into pond scum
Kaleidoscopes of blood and pus
No one touches the zombie
Pelted with combustible rocks

Except paramedics parkouring up the stairs
Don't get up Nancy
When the sun doesn't shine and the wind doesn't blow
You can be sure the board will be starjumping
On TikTok

Incidentally at the wharf
Tuna shovelled into utes
Will fly carbon far
No further than all the seas of a lifetime

That four-letter word at this point
Can Only Articulate Lust
Black gold blackouts

Black Angel's Death Song

They've lost him lost count of him I mean
Christmas card replaced by Hello All
The bottom line of excuses signed off

Old coal miner's going nowhere
Because Nancy won't leave the wheelchair
Frozen lasagne and Rocky Road
From a Woolies truck. Electric?
Not until battery is a prospectus

Another fall at night phone out of reach
In the empty moaning dawn
Old coal miner manages to place the call
Taken in with Nancy finally at the hourly rate

Busy brother appears much later
Pulls down the stair lift for Ebay
Furniture piled out the front

Dingo prowls from the backyard orchard
Eyes like glowing lemons
Shameful in his treachery
Treacherous in his shame to that point where
Peace and freedom come in the act of killing

THE PAST

Sometimes I feel like I've been waiting
For the past to catch up
In a good way
Still, does that make me an imposter?
But then I turn on a dark road going home
And there he is
Eminem in a hoodie at a bus stop or Sam Shepard
Waiting by a ute load of firewood on the shoulder
And the bus comes and goes
And I feel I should be on the bus
Or Shepard climbs in the ute
Lights a cigarette and roars away
And I don't have enough firewood

All those other stories I wrote
In all those towns and cities
All given voice for a moment
But a moment may have been enough
To be heard
To lament or exalt
And if those stories were told again
End to end they might reach a chosen star
Or at least Orbost
But they are gone into stardust
I remember outlines glowing in the dark
And I suspect those stories may remember me
Does that make me a thief?

The last time I turned for home
I felt like the *Girl With A Pearl Earring*

And my bright green Dragster
Had packed up and gone
Rolling into a forest and I followed
Guessing this may be why the past never
Catches up because the past is moving
In another direction, to escape
And is careful
Does that make me lost?

My later stories are much the same
In that respect, keeping the past
At arm's length and sometimes I wonder
If this is the purpose of the past
Yesterday I saw the past in my local deli
Her hair was purple and she wore a nose ring
She smiled and winked at me before riding away
And I felt more or less at ease
But still somehow tricked

ON 'YURL YURL', ANYA JUDITH SAMSON

Martu Country
with respect

Deepest is the blood red
eyeless face
cupped handless
in olive and cream
above or below five rings
intense and younger
a processional
for the dark red Munchian
ellipse voicing
not *The Scream*
in activated dreamscape
far beyond
an undignified suffering

THE DOLLS

This madhouse has three floors, all glass.
You can touch the dolls, if you want to keep the spell.
Dolls are fallen deities of the moon.
At night, when we dream, dolls become flesh.
Of course they do, and for better or worse, mind.
For a doll to play with power is a dangerous thing.

Serafina, wooden, Italian maid, 1920s,
layered aprons, faded gingham and lace,
white buttoned collar, chipped pink lips,
thick black eyebrows, black shellac hair, middle part,
age anywhere. Thirty? Fifty? Faint knowing smile.
Italian but in the circus a flamenco dancer,
fell hard for the strongman in leopard skin,
dropped like an acrobat,
found in the back room of a Braidwood café
slouched in a cupboard with two friends or lovers
drowsy with opium. I paid for Serafina
wrapped in light blue tissue paper.

Dolls are hunters, merciless and territorial, like magpies.
We are the chosen but we are not special.
A standing doll never blinks.
Doll gaze is bad energy
projecting the weight of desire.

Freddy, wooden, articulated mannequin, also 1920s,
for a prominent bohemian in the Munich salons,
retrieved from an asylum on the psychiatrist's desk.
Head cocked, affronted by Serafina

lounging at his side, Freddy cannot say no
when the dark comes and she lifts her skirt
to straddle him and writhe.

I had promised Serafina to Giovanni but it didn't work out.
Giovanni, also 1920s, also Italian, also wooden, head only,
tatty muslin coat, dirty hand puppet
picked sneering from an antiques barn in Brunswick Heads.
Short, sharp, black devil beard, bold red eyes,
black hair cropped low on the forehead.
Giovanni pimps the Barbies, those Malibu bitches
lying all day on the pool chaise, easy chair,
plastic radio, another Slim Aarons tableau.
Giovanni is out of his league with Serafina,
who knows they may one day marry.

Elvis Costello saw it coming, beyond the night,
a doll revolution.
Dolls in the Martian Embassy. Dolls in the Kremlin.
Sex and drugs and dolls.

Big doll Clara Julia is in love with me.
English, 1950s, box of costumes.
Currently Sunyassin, wants to be Christina Hendricks.
Clara Julia is a jealous thief, steals credit cards,
redeemed by cascading strawberry blonde hair.
Three months in a wardrobe with the Chairman Mao
bust from a Beijing flea market, completely unhinged.
Not uncommon for dolls but traumatic nonetheless.
Overmedicated hairdresser gave us Pauly,
in a sailor's suit and cap, like Lou Reed.
Darling, take him. I can't bear him any longer.
We sent Pauly to Clara Julia's op shop,
kept his stand, a metal rod and a metal collar.

Clara Julia wears it now, doing better.
Dolls do not data mine or plagiarise reason.
Dolls do not mock our words.
Dolls will never work for us.
Dolls do not follow the rule of law.
Dolls are bat shit crazy.

In Lagos and the Philippines, dolls live openly.
Dolls control the Republican Party.
Dolls control the Conservative Party.
Dolls control the Liberal National Coalition.
Rudi Giuliani. Doll. Michaela Cash. Doll.
Ivana Trump. Doll. Barnaby Joyce. Doll. Boris Johnson. Doll.
Donald's hands. From a doll. Peter Dutton. Head of a doll.

Nelson's body was put in a brandy cask
mixed with camphor and myrrh, lashed to *Victory's* mast.
At Greenwich, the body was placed in a wooden coffin
from the mast of the *L'Orient*, salvaged from the Battle of the Nile.
Taken on a barge upriver, lay in state at the Admiralty,
escorted by 10,000 soldiers to St Paul's, four-hour service,
sarcophagus in a crypt, the uncompleted tomb of Henry VIII.
All documented, less understood is the resurrection.
Those Staffordshire figurines.

I found Nelson at Portsmouth, on The Hard,
not far from the tailor who stitched his last uniform.
In the madhouse, Nelson waits at the feet
of Queen Lilu'uokolani, last Hawaiian monarch,
seated as a child on a high scallop back cane chair
from a cardboard box beside a recycled clothing bin.
Black afro, white lipstick, straw bra, bare stomach,
white grass skirt, white grass choker, white shoes.
Throne usurped, campaign failed, Lilu refuses to speak.
Lady Hamilton all but forgotten, Nelson can only whisper:

I never knew, I never knew.
Oh, puzzled Lord, forgive us. At Milan, in *The Last Supper*
we saw dolls under the table eating scraps.

MORE USES FOR THE BOTTLEBRUSH FLOWER

*From the kitchen diary of Mrs Alice Sullivan, overseer's wife, Country
Women's Association district past president, Wandilago Station, New South
Wales, 1926*

Harold says it's been a long summer
I should spend more time in the shade
This morning I waited in the machinery shed
I could see the men in the shadows
Hear their talk like fire crackle and soft hands

Dough roller shoe tree bird comb

A visit from the crow
Another black menace at the fly screen door
Staring like them all at my soul
I gave him a bite of mutton
A sip of the blood of Christ
He was ungrateful

Honey dipper cupboard duster earrings

The mare in the top paddock got away
Dug a tunnel under the fence at Sunday lunch
I took the lucerne and made a crumble with raisins

Possum poker hair coiler soup stirrer

This cursed weather
I wore nothing but the flour sack apron
Excelsior brand
I told Harold on my back
I felt the breath of Zeus

Cobweb catcher potato scrubber snake sword

I saw them early lined up on the ridge
Embryo fingers curled and glowing
Charles and Ern and Arthur
Burning with excitement
Finally home from the war
It won't be long now

Back scratcher mosquito trap cream whisker

CULTURAL WASTELAND

Kingsford Smith in the cockpit
threads the memorial gate at Bega
to examine for the royal commission
troubling reports
broadcast handsfree from supersize
chariots of contempt
burning non-renewable self-interest rates

an absence
of sensitive attunement to pictures
and nowhere recommended to eat
quelle horreur
a cultural wasteland

the privileged flippers
refuse to respect pictures
limping on the street
rat tails marked with blue teardrops
trailing perfect bare feet children

confining difference and disadvantage
to contactless causes
god forbid close encounters
the worthless speculators
are impelled to paint *something*
before lunch on the restaurant terrace
blue bottled tap water
hummingbird cake
in small bites and sips

the daredevil goes anywhere
but is a poor rapporteur
he cannot see from above
steep contours of wealth
attendant drones with lifelines
only silhouettes in a red wave

he shakes his wings at the skatepark
turns up sharp and is swallowed
by cheesy cloud
no findings for prosecution
no place for barnstorming
where the coastal floppers
cannot comprehend
unrenovated stucco

the regional art gallery still closed
probably a good thing
easier to ignore

Fred McCubbin on the edge of town
sketches drowsy bunyips
under Mumbulla

THE BEGINNING OF THE END #1

Ron the time ticker has run along weaving down among the Union Street scenes and shimmering beams only miles away from power base lefts under the arch. Alcatraz is part of the art. A way to start this wizening dream on a run to there and back, always in black, Jack. Say shake a voo, belly rubs, too, muttering palpitations for tomorrow and the next day means nothing or could be eons away and further to the generator song of Tom. It's all been so long gone but that's not what's anywhere near today. To go someday and put this plot inside your play, games can chance you any other way. And hex the jex of any sex who wove itself on cobwebs moribund round the rally go boys for the bubble of the toiling trouble has gone to pot. What to say is no man's fray, unwelcome and oblique. Obscure caricatures bending any way you want after late movies while the rings are gold. Change can shame and dismiss impervious crap, so we lie asky all wrought and wry and try to see the light. Tonight. But the sun will shimmy shally all just a day away. So now you know the way to go, on Geary near Hyde. So does Clyde. He plays electric bass, he's off the planet, face, too, see if you do. Commenting earlier this week on Reagan's budget proposals, with some of the biggest spending cuts in history, budget director David Stockman said the thundering herd of sacred cows has been reduced to a handful.

THE BEGINNING OF THE END #2

Close the doors and kick away the lice, take a train and grab your brain, the game is not yet finished, wait, run fast and soon you might be free. I hate casual attire. Dress up for me this evening. Then he says, I'm going to have a menage a trois with twins. They lead to wailing sirens and a man with jet blue hair exclaims, oh my god, I'm being framed. Flushing sure beats brushing. He says, I've got Dina and Nina all lined up. I am dreaming of Marilyn. She lifts her skirt and splashes through puddles. Marilyn, I would chase you in the rain. I would cry under streetlamps. I would play with my food and swim behind your iris. The scheme of things is Stiff Little Fingers. You must stay low in the fast lane. We may puke at our depravity, reneg and revile our passions. There is no passion. What happens when rapture meets passion? Go to Mars, eat guitars, play Cadillacs and drive bars. Katherine is elegant with the grace of an unbranded calf, or as Ernie says, like a deer grazing in a field. She graduated from a walking stick to two and then a four-pronged aluminium frame she could lean on and tug at and finally a chair. But when she arched her back straining to take in the city and ran her hands down her hips, well, I might have believed she was 25.

THE BEGINNING OF THE END #3

The risk that one or more advisors will die here grows every day. They take precautions but they are obvious targets for assassins. They vary the route from their quarters to their assignments and when not on duty they carry pistols and dress in civilian clothes. But some have already had their pictures published and as they continue their six month tours their habits and whereabouts will inevitably become known. There is also a risk of serious accidents. One advisor was walking out of a San Salvador restaurant when his friend dropped a loaded pistol, which shot him through the foot. I am drinking a glass of water. As the water runs out of the bathroom tap it bounces onto the bottom of the glass and disappears into airy, sudsy bubbles up the sides to the top, all dark grey foam. When the tap is turned off the bubbles stretch out and burst onto themselves, leaving a rim of particles around the edge, wearing thin. Like old thongs. State Department spokesman William Dyers said the attackers were diseased. A guerilla group of Costa Ricans who fought with the Sandinistas claimed responsibility for the blast in a communique to a San Jose radio station. They said the attack demonstrated the solidarity of the Salvadoran people. An anonymous phone tip led to the evacuation of the embassy six minutes before the explosion.

THE BEGINNING OF THE END #4

Welcome to the syndrome. His client Rodriquez is emotional although he holds it within. There are a lot of problems. The jury in total supports that, by their notes. Mrs Harris is guilty of murder. She loved him and now she has iron around her wrists. I did not wish him ill. With a gun. Several rows of spectators broke into applause. No possibility of parole until 1996. The State's only maximum-security prison for women. It is not a happy time. *The Enquirer* is slashing Carol Burnett. They catch up with you eventually. I can't say chivalry, but now it is written. Witty, number nineteen, confident, number nineteen, outspoken, number nineteen, and a federally funded giveaway is picking up steam. It is the burro's only chance. Looks like it is going to be another hot year. There's only one thing that can happen when they run out of food and that is, they will die. We raise them and we sell them. Much easier together. When he gets in a crowd, he's satisfied. Competing together, they are spoken for. Coal will be crippled longer than a walkout and bankruptcy buys up the fields. Now they want all the coal. Their masters want them to break the union, to break the smaller operators, who will pick up the pieces of coal. A group of representatives. Leave the president some flexibility. What're you gonna do? Listen to the looks of strangers? Remember Dylan wanted to jump the fallout shelter. It was a very eerie experience, that last bit, by the way. I mean, it really was something I'd never been through before, but it wasn't, Christ, what can you relate it to? I dunno. The situation was well done. It was 4.30 in the morning. You looked at those guys' faces, you couldn't see their eyes. The bullets were handed out. It was calm. I felt an incredible calm. The stillness. Australians and Americans are similar. We're probably not as confused. The pincer is a new phase of a three-week campaign in the north. Army patrols backed by planes and helicopters have been conducting sweeps.

SILENT COUNSELLOR

I'm out of town, on the Childers road
for my unscheduled drive by consultation.
There you are, crown glowing in the winter sunset
alone in a radiant pasture.
Your aloneness makes you familiar.
I slow down, roll the window
reassured by a thousand green hands
breathing backwards on another frequency
plumes of comfort and sustenance.
My unspoken confession
to the patience of your seeds.
Your wordless advice: be yourself, hasten slowly, listen
avoid anything sudden
like the aim of reckless jackeroos.
So many more of you
forgive our repeated mistakes and indiscretions.
The many of us not enough to know your waiting
may not save you.
I smile at the old Holden
rusty under your shade without an epitaph
all those ants in the tank
rise to the tarnished sky.

WEDDING TREE

After I climbed the pine at Kaikoura
You said yes
You said that was the clincher
I was not fleeing the aggressive seals
You knew I wouldn't leave you
On the rocks

I learned fast
Alarm clocks, Thai basil, perfume
On a brass tray with dragons
Shaven in chinos, suede and linen
You said thank you and I'll go there
And you took me swaying
To St Hippolyte de Montaigu

To a table under the midsummer Mimosa
Rosé, Bach and bees
Leaf shadows nuzzling
The baguette and the fricassee
When the rain came the drops
On our side of the curtain gave us time

For waiting out the silences
If not for the rats under our feet
The boy painting lipstick on the carpet
Measuring power and control
Until the trunk was full again
And we sipped together
In a cradle of limbs

Ed Southorn was a newspaper reporter for 32 years in capital cities and country towns across Australia and in England. He taught journalism in Queensland universities for a decade. His poetry, narrative journalism, short fiction and memoir have appeared in *Cordite Poetry Review, Axon: Creative Explorations, Meniscus, Blackbox Manifold, The Journal of Wild Culture, Moveable Type, The Ekphrastic Review*, NSW South Coast Writers Centre anthologies and elsewhere. His PhD explores contested space. His MPhil is a history of surfing. He has hitchhiked across America and is a foundation member of the Gold Coast Surf World museum. He lives at Bermagui.